I0799065

Rag Bits

by Greg Frazier
illustrated by Olivia Cole

Core Decodable 26

McGraw Hill Education

Bothell, WA • Chicago, IL • Columbus, OH • New York, NY

MHEonline.com

Send all inquiries to:
McGraw-Hill Education
8787 Orion Place
Columbus, OH 43240

ISBN: 978-0-02-143438-1
MHID: 0-02-143438-7

Printed in Canada.

9 10 11 12 KOD 24

Mom had a big bag.

The bag had a tag.

"Grab the bag and look," said Mom.

Nan had a plan.
Nan got the bag.

Mom was a pig fan.
Nan had a rag gift.

Mom got a pig gift.
It was a pig flag.